river
woman

also by katherena vermette

POETRY
North End Love Songs

FICTION
The Break

CHILDREN'S LITERATURE
The Seven Teachings Stories Series
A Girl Called Echo Series

river
woman

katherena vermette

ANANSI

Published in Canada in 2018 and the USA in 2018 by House of Anansi Press Inc.
www.houseofanansi.com

House of Anansi Press is committed to protecting our natural environment. As part of our efforts, the interior of this book is printed on paper made from second-growth forests and is acid-free.

22 21 20 19 18   1 2 3 4 5

Library and Archives Canada Cataloguing in Publication

Vermette, Katherena, 1977–, author
River woman / Katherena Vermette.

Poems.
Issued in print and electronic formats.
ISBN 978-1-4870-0346-3 (softcover).—ISBN 978-1-4870-0348-7 (hardcover).—
ISBN 978-1-4870-0347-0 (EPUB).—ISBN 978-1-4870-0626-6 (Kindle)

I. Title.

PS8643.E74R59 2018   C811'.6   C2018-900061-9
                                             C2018-900062-7

Library of Congress Control Number: 2018931738

Cover artwork: *Red River 1870s (beaded map)* (2006) by David Garneau; collection of the Murray Library, University of Saskatchewan
Cover design: Sara Loos
Text design and typesetting: Laura Brady

Canada Council   Conseil des Arts   ONTARIO ARTS COUNCIL
for the Arts   du Canada   CONSEIL DES ARTS DE L'ONTARIO
                                            an Ontario government agency
                                            un organisme du gouvernement de l'Ontario

We acknowledge for their financial support of our publishing program the Canada Council for the Arts, the Ontario Arts Council, and the Government of Canada.

Printed and bound in Canada

MIX
Paper from
responsible sources
FSC   FSC® C004071
www.fsc.org

For Reuben

contents

"I assert that poetry without politics is narcissistic and not useful to us. I also believe that everything is political — there is no neutral safe place we can hide out in waiting for the brutality to go away."

— Chrystos

black river

"Like the river flows
  Surely to the sea,
  Darling so it goes,
  Some things were meant to be."
                        — Elvis Presley

pieces

we fit
like small
puzzle pieces
tiny things
who together
create a whole

like two
pieces of shard glass
whose seams seem
to fuse

and if we
hold them
there
they look
like they were never
broken

breathe

we breathe fresh
air into our suffocated
selves and speak
long Anishnaabemowin
words I trace
across your skin
our scars stretched
to their edges

smooth Anishnaabemowin
words move in
and out of time
waft through
our bodies as sure as
smudge

every word beautiful
when it falls off
your lips
when I catch it
with mine
when your kiss
lingers long there

river

river dances
out to lake
lake rushes back
to river
waters wash
around each other
and change

two people
couple
a batter whipped
smooth ingredients
that together
make something
new

lake

but in november when
waves freeze
into crooked
fingers
beckon us
out onto untouched
ground

in november when
the lake becomes
white with
rough mounds
like old graves
open
calling

black river

fog tumbled
all around the highway that
very mild winter
february wet
and warm
your heat vents
set low
you drove slow

look at this
you said
look
night spread out
we listened to all our favourite songs
sang and held hands
because you didn't have to shift gears
on the highway
look!

the light-smudged sky
a wooly blanket
on either side of us
trees heavy with hoar frost

we're going to remember this
you said
and turned down the music
to say the words
one day

you're going to tell our kids
this one time I was driving up to black river with your dad . . .

you laughed
but I could almost see it
a whole life
laid out before us
as sure as the flat
Manitoba earth

only hidden
as if by fog

ghosts

1.

ghosts linger
on our clothes
mean ones
haunt
the folds of our blanket
take flight
when I shake it out
to make the bed

they fly around the room
hide in corners
crouch in shadows
watch us
wait

to stretch their hands
over our shoulders
pull small words
out of our mouths
and fluff them like pillows
until they are so big
they block our eyes

dance between us
make faces
their laughs echo

until we can't hear
anything but them

and we forget
who we are even talking to
or who we get to love now

2.

ghosts stuck on our skins
the cruel ones
taunting
dirty

we need to
wrap each other'
in warm water
soak our tired bodies
like wet earth in spring
we need to fill up
until we spill out

until pools surround
us like aura
and we can drift
our weighted hands
toward each other
lift them
out of water
the only tears
off our fingertips

and we can finally
wash our wounds

if they could be
at peace

if we could be
so still
so still
the ripples soften
around us

tongues

tongues laced in
stories move
in and out of everything
nothing
is inanimate

tongues tied in
sacred words
transcend ceremony
into every
day

tongues knotted in
verbs long and wanting
to be understood
meaning shape
shifts

its context
out of past
tense and renewed
each time

scars

1.

scars glare
like glyphs
on walls long dark
uncovered
by light

lines etched on
skin white
against brown
marks imposed
curved

a script to decipher
slow
a story of another
time

2.

lines emboss
once-smooth skin
tattooed secrets
read like code

spoken with hand
crooked to ear
breath hot
against lobe

did you
know
we should have
known
this

arch

night
comes as
comfortable
as a bed as
cumbersome
as limbs as soft
as an arch to put
your hand under
as rich as a slice
of moon so sweet
you have to spoon
me small rounded
bites I nibble slow
and savour in long
languid mouthfuls
lapping my tongue
around their texture
a taste so beautiful
I miss it before
I even
swallow

a fine dust

we are so close
I can only see
you in pinpoints
fine
sharp

I am so close
I can hear the breath
between my words
those small
quiet spaces
too short
not safe
enough

I know you so well
I don't know you at all

you are only
the songs I hum
when no one is near
a story I can recite
by heart
but don't understand

you break me
shatter the pieces
left
I have become

a fine dust
I can so easily
blow away

you know me so well
you don't know me at all

speak

speak
talk
listen
be
silent
as
the
lake
in
winter

I missed it
freezing
now it's
cold
and quiet
as a

don't
speak
don't
talk
or
whisper
hear them
wind
trees
talk to each other

ghosts
speak stories
the ones that
come
off the lake
dance
through
the bush
fall on our
hair
those stories

now speak
talk
whisper
sing
listen
listen
don't forget to
listen

Anishnaabemowin

I take out the book
at night when
we sit together
quiet
5 I want to learn the language
I should have known
my tongue trips
over double vowels
like feet
10 in shoes too big

I remember
words as
intangible as
dreams
15 so real
at night
but I can't quite
grasp them
in the day

cocoon

cocooned in
winter white
I slip beside you
breathe deep

if you listen
you can hear the snow
change
shift slow to spring
poised for melt

cloaked under
white winter
I lie beside you
breathe out

if you listen
you can hear
wet wings unfurl
like petals
ready to be
born

inches

we move in
inches
not leaps
or bounds
time is different
here

we gesture
together
then apart
again
left
somewhere
quite small
only a little
beyond where
we were

but we feel it
in our bones
in the sinew-skin of our intertwined
fingers
when we walk
under the elms
where buds bring out
their almost
green

when we sigh

into the marrow of
a quiet Saturday
stay in
blend closer

but then
something
and we go
so very far away
again
coil back
a bit
again
before

we move
in inches

crowfight

have you ever seen a crowfight?
from down here
it looks like a dance
a courtship
how they swoop
and curve around
each other

you'd think it was love

but their claws are out
their cries fierce
they sweep
and curl
take turns
chase each other
across the sky

it almost looks like
us

broken

because we are
broken
there are cracks
in us
where the dark
gets in

we only hold
ourselves
together
let go
and we fall
let go
and we come
a part

red river

"A nation is not conquered until the hearts of its women are in the ground.
Then it is finished, no matter how brave its warriors or how strong their weapons."
— A saying from the Cheyenne people

ziibiwan (like a river)

1.

she is
born atop
a long lake
called Traverse
rises between
two territories
Dakota
Anishnaabe
she is
both
and neither

her modest beginnings
in the south
more like a creek
gentle but
she pushes
ever north
she is
border
road
source
saviour

she is
river
like
and not

2.

near the 49th
land gets large
and she widens
like memory
grows strong
tempestuous
dips into
low valley
quick
fastidious
forward

she is
the healing
not the hurt

she is
the knowing
not unknown

3.

the city makes her quiet
contemplative
cold
her brown skin
holds rumour
voices carry
over her body

her turns both
mindful
instinctive
nothing can stop her
some have tried
but all have
failed

we can only
make room
lay down tobacco
and love her
as she's been
waiting to
be

4.

near the lake
the locks comb her
out she roars
over them
insulted
to be so
encumbered
beyond them

she stretches out
into the grassland
marshes
pelicans rest
gulls call
to her slowing
spirit
if you only knew her
up here
you'd think she was
at peace

5.

she grows
low
clear as
the lake
her child
who looks nothing
like her

she is blue now
as sky at twilight
as eyes wise enough
to be kind
she is if only
she is as if
lapis lazuli
and sapphire
had a beautiful baby
girl

river woman

this river is a woman
she is bright
and she is beautiful
she once carried
every nation here
but she is
one of those women
too soon forgotten
broken like a body
that begs without words
only rough hands
that reach out
palms up

this river is a woman
she's been dredged
and dragged
metal coils catch
her tangled hair
everyone wants to know
her secrets but
she keeps them
won't let them go
unless she trusts you
unless you ask real nice
unless she
feels like it

this river is a woman
she's full of

good intentions
bad regrets
sometimes she just folds
into herself
can slow to a slush
then rush into race
currents indiscernible
patterns intangible
and below
she goes even
faster

this river is a woman
forever
returning
twisting north
a snake carved
into prairie grass
hiding everywhere
eroded with age
etched into her edges
and newly born
every day

this river is your lover
she curls around
you pulses
and fills you
like a heartbeat
if you are very quiet

all you hear is her

this river is your mother
she flows on and on
and unnoticed
slips in
slides out
as if she was never here
as if she were always here

this river is my sister
she is bright and beautiful
and brown
sings soft every summer
holds us up all winter
and every spring she swells
reminds us we are just
visitors here
this is her country
she is that woman
her deft voice
reaches out
broken by everything that has been
thrown into her
but
somehow her spirit
rages on
somehow a song
like her
never fades

riveredge

1.

the river is so low
too low
for so early in the season
broken beams
of a long-forgotten dock
stick out of the water
geese nest
between them
their long necks intertwine
wings stretch out
over warm eggs

2.

gulls cry
between the bridges
surf tiny white waves
peck at new bugs

they sound like cats
and turn like fish
confident
able
fearless

3.

crows caw
from the fallen
trees eroded white
first by winter
then by water
tilted toward the earth
like they snapped
apart
gave up
and now lie there
waiting
for the river
to take them

riverdawn

still as glass
flies dance across
her mirrored surface
their tiny treads sprinkle
across the reflection
like rain

the pink in the sky
hardens
sun opens over dark trees
fading the slip of a waning moon
and the last lip of smoky dew
burns off the grass

where ducks call
push out to greet the day
their ripples stretch far
across water
blur the clouds

riverevening

dusk as slow as
heartbreak

river laps in lisps
against dock

stills to a sleep
grey and long

sun sinks
trees turn

I miss you
forever

there are so many
to miss

riverlove

I've sat along this river
most of my life
but rarely went

in a boat
to sit atop
and rock upon her
until the current swayed
in my blood
the movement rushed
under my skin

now that I know her
I sit here high on the grass
and feel her with me
she laps slower
but ripples in my chest
like love
it is love
that's what love is

riverstory

I search
for stories of the river
scratch at the surface
dig deep
pull at bits of limestone
and other forgotten things
but I can't find them
those things that we were never supposed to
lose

I wait
to hear the stories of the river
sit at the edge
scoop up the silence
my fingers tangle
in the long dark hair
there is always long dark hair
that is where our spirits linger
left behind to wander the waves

I need to hear
the stories of the river
about when she was young
and her brown water was
clean
loved

riverlocks

nothing gets through
but through them

the locks at St Andrews
are closed all summer
to keep the river steady
and open from October
to late June
to force the flow

when the ice freezes
and expands
when it breaks in spring
pieces as big as islands
push up against
the locks at St Andrews

because nothing gets through
but through them

where

not up in the groomed grass
of the pretty park

not in the hilly bush
high with growth and garbage

not kneeling
on those polished pews

not even where the upright stones
bruise the earth

not at the street where
the fake flowers faded long ago

or where wounds open
and cry out every night

not on the bridge where
some went

or at old wood dock where
others were taken

but here near this last bend
in the river

here where the trees break off
and their leaves dance high with song

here where the water licks the sky
like smoke

and the concrete is so old
and smoothed as rock

here where the dock broke off
and the edge is low

where the wind moves quick in
and long out

there is still tobacco
and there is still fire

here with the river is where
I will remember

riversong

sing your humble
melody
your wandering
water sound

cry out your song
so we can follow
that tender tune

strum the current
like strings

wake earth
with truth

I hear you
my sister
sing
sing

riverceremony

however we go
she holds us close
washes us
like ceremony

it doesn't matter
that she was so greedy
she never gave us all
back

when I die
whether I fall
or go
give me to her
in thanks
in ceremony

if I am with her
I am home
she can keep me
as long as she wants
she can keep me as she has
forever

this river

for the Red River

this river is old
her story is long
this river is wide
and open

but this river is broken
she is like the pillars of old piers
the ones that stick out of the water
at the shore
lapped over by every wake
you can't always see
but she is always there

this river is ignored
people cross the street to avoid this river
they pretend they meant to go that way all along but
you can tell by the hunch in their shoulders
no one wants to be anywhere near
this river

this river is so
inconvenient
they had to make bridges to cut across her
inconsistent bends
straight lines to make up for all her
dangerous curves

this river is a dump
a waste
her only abundance is garbage
and blue smudges
iridescent in the sun
shining oil as it surfaces
from the sludge below

this river is like that crumbling dock
the one caution taped off and fenced away
left to rot
they will tear it down as soon as they can
one day when
they think we are not looking
they will pull it apart
and take all the pieces away
without a word

but this river is smart
street smart and book smart
this river has learned and been schooled
this river is so well read she's worn out

this river is a trickster
she can lick her lips
smile you closer
and just when you think you have her
she puffs black smoke
and laps off into her next form

how irrational is this river
this river is a bitch in a mood
she won't let you
throw anchor
where you want to
won't let you go
'cause you want to

but this river is sweet
she can be so gentle
so beauty full
she is a water carrier
after all

she is a masterpiece
with the wondering eyes of Norval Morrisseau
the wandering hands of Daphne Odjig

she is love
she is the eagles soaring above the trees
she is power pushing pure
north

this river is the reason we are all here
she carried us all
on her broad brown back
without complaint
this river's only payment has been our refuse
refusals
indifference

but this river
doesn't need your attention or your inquiry
this river is too busy
doing what she has always done —
kicking ass and taking care
this river has never been idle
she was here before you
and she will be here
long after we've all
gone

this river is full
this river is family
this river is forever
because this river
of course
is red

an other story

"The river is immense, and it has the capacity to receive, embrace and transform. If our hearts are big, we can be like the river."
— Thich Nhat Hanh

an other story

this country has an other story
one that is not his
or hers
or ours

it is written
in water
carved on earth
every stone
a song
that echoes
the erosion
hold one
to your ear
whispers
rise

this country has another story
and it is not his
or hers
or even ours

it is scrolled on wind
painted in blood
every bone
sings
hold them
to your heart

those buried voices
still
rise

new year's eve 2013

1.

people are dancing
on Portage and Main
like they danced there
500 years ago

Elders starve for words
settlers refuse to give
trolls circle their wagons
across the internet frontier
injuns! they cry
arguments fired off
with more fear than precision

they don't understand
in this place
truth is a seed
planted deep

if you want to get it
you have to dig

2.

they say all people were created equal
who cannot agree
I say I will believe it
when prison and poverty rates are the same
when thousands of your women disappear
and you do nothing

these things are not equal
the world is unfair
we all have to pull ourselves up
by our own bootstraps
make something of ourselves

but what about those who don't
have boots

dear settler
you get to pretend your ancestors
weren't given free land
a good start
strong equipment
hand outs
your grandparents took with begging hands
and help
from neighbouring indians
who knew
how to
hunt

make
plant
you get to pretend it didn't happen like this
but it did

we can't pretend
it doesn't matter

3.

we are not a part of your mosaic
we are the mortar that glues you together
we are the foundation on which you adhere
we are the earth you are hurting
no
you cannot do what you will with her
she never belonged to you
she is as
church
synagogue
mosque and Mecca
these places do not belong to any of us

4.

I am Métis
part of all parts
my people knew
how to make this work
they left instruction in our culture
our clothing woven by the looms of my grandmothers
bone needles sewed beads into
European florals and sharp Anishnaabe lines
moccassined feet danced to fiddles

they hunted and fished both ways
prayed and sang both ways
their words moving
in and out of both languages

it was supposed to be
like this

5.

right over there
where rivers meet
people have always met
500 years is nothing
this place is too deep
this earth is a living history
we are honoured to walk upon

don't you understand
truth is a seed
planted deep

you can't get it
unless you dig

people are dancing
on Portage and Main
like they danced there
500 years ago
like they will dance there
in 500 more

uncarved

name plates
under statues
each prime minister
every explorer
discoverer
their faces carved
with precision
eyes modelled in perfect
resemblance

Indigenous statues
only have tribal names
Iroquois
Mohawk
Algonquin
under imagined faces
probable regalia
they grow green
with age
their names
stories
histories
uncarved

another winter

when we walked
through the snow
in Ottawa

your feet blistered
from the rented shoes
but you walked with me anyway

to the gallery
across the bridge
to the museum

the cold wind of winter
coming
but everything was good
and every photo funny

now I walk
across Winnipeg
in a snowstorm

the city muffled
quiet
white

winter finally
decidedly
arrived

my feet are strong
and warm
I can walk
far

but you're not here
but you're not here

how to argue

remember your love's best self
remember your best self
only let
the two of them talk
think of love
and all the dreams you share

don't walk away

take a break
if you need to
choose your words
carefully
do not punish
do not blame

never use the word
never
or always
think of what you want
not only how you feel

don't run away

learn to breathe
learn to trust
your love is true
even when you are angry
your love is full

even when you are empty

don't say things you don't mean
don't let insecurity convince you
of something that is not true
arguing is still talking
resolution is possible

believe in yourself
believe in your love
hold on

don't go away

I come from a place that

is the centre of the world
right here in a middle
it sits like a water bug
on the back of a turtle
lost in the slick
shifting colours
of its shell
and the moons there

is so cold
no one ever settled here
in the winter
that season found them
moved to its far edges
protected by bush
not until the stubborn Métis
and only because they had
no other place to go

was once the bottom
a great ocean
water spread over the whole
country
then dried as mysteriously
as it had filled

so hot in the summer
the grass yellows
so cold in the winter

you can freeze in minutes
this place
has tried every degree
so unsatisfied
it keeps shifting

of three rivers
but not the one in Quebec
one river is no more than a creek
named grandly
by the French who "discovered" it
and called it Seine
it weaves a curvy line southeast
and trickles down
into nothing

another river
Assiniboine
comes in from the west
like the people its named after
it is as gentle
as a strand of hair
smoothed to a curl

the biggest river is Red
though no one knows why
it comes from a small lake in the south
unassuming until it picks up
speed and strength
to the grand inland ocean

the remnant of something
once bigger

   where planted trees arch avenues
align our little lives
with shade
and century-old buildings tell
the story of a different city
a hopeful one

   whose first story
is one of resistance
though they called it
a rebellion

   where some people thrive
many die
where choices are limited
and nothing much was ever
expected of me

   where loved ones
go missing almost every day

   where I won't let my daughters
walk down many streets
even with someone
or take a cab

where thunderbirds cry
and wind sings lullabies
trees whisper stories
rivers ripple verse
and talk to each other
all night long
but never listen

with more contradictions
than this poem

where Elders are kicked out
for loitering one month
and honoured with a headdress
the next

that smells like smudge
and cigarettes
and cold air somehow
never far away
even in August
especially in August

so brutal and beautiful
hard to understand
even harder to forgive
but somehow so easy
to love

métissage / Métis Sage

1.

métissage

my blood has been here forever
as rooted as the river
and just as in danger

this body has pounded
prairie and pemmican
plodded and considered
every hill and hole

we are nothing less
than the whole stretched-out sky
nothing more
than the loose hair that dances in it

2.

Ontario goes on
and on
a day and a half by train
evergreens an uninterrupted
blur with only
brief breaks for power lines
broken-down houses
sky

it's easy to see how big
they thought it must be
green seems to be never ending
it's easy to see how
they thought they wouldn't ever
have to stop
taking

3.

fur trade was the first
industry they brought
this country was made for it
thick with brown
bison
so huge their migrations indented
the very prairie beneath them

it only took
two hundred years
to hunt them to near extinction
the beaver too
skinned for trendy top hats
until they too
went out of style
and sea otters have never been seen since
it only took
two hundred years
to have so little left
many First Peoples starved
hung out to dry
like the once-priceless skins
now sold for pennies

next was the railroad
easier to make in a country
not a colony
so nationalism was born

Canada bought it all
from the Hudson's Bay Company
for next to nothing
the "empty" excess sold for more
but only to European immigrants

profits made this country
railroad reached the other ocean
settlers flooded
for cheap land and donated food
the only "free" in this country
for them

4.

it is not history
it has not passed
there is nothing to get over
it is still happening
this land is still used up
for all it can give
our mother abused
the only thing they think she is good for
an oil sand field as big as Scotland
every river mined for Hydro
earth and water
polluted with commercial farms
and that ever-green of Ontario
is being cut down faster
than it can be sold

5.

Métis Sage

my blood has been here forever
as rooted as the river
and just as much in danger

this body has pounded
prairie and pemmican
plodded and considered
every hill and hole

we are nothing less
than the whole stretched-out sky
nothing more
than the loose hair that dances in it

my blood has been here forever
as long as the land
and just as unprotected

when Louis Riel went crazy

1.

after the Red River "Rebellion" of 1869
Louis Riel went crazy
he ran off and hid
in a bush along the Seine
a land that jutted
out into the stream
a place everyone called
Vermette's point
just a thick
mass of thin trees
next to a narrow
slot of ploughed land
meek farm house
a brief place
nondescript
but the prideful home of my great-
great uncle and aunt

Riel stayed there a month
a long month when
spring spread out slowly
separated him from his "crimes"
I imagine my aunt left food for him
at the bush's edge
bannock lard and meat on an old tin plate
a meal for a dog
or a "rebel"

something he would have to hurry to
so the foxes didn't get there first

some say that's where Louis took
the name David where
in his cold hungry penitence
God spoke to him
gave him his divine purpose
and a middle name

when Louis Riel was hanged in 1885
my great-great uncle had no land
Manitoba had become a province
Canadian surveyors came in
and Métis homesteads were dissected
bisected
halved
quartered
over and over again until
nothing was left
only a square to balance one foot on
for only one second
before they all fell over

Ottawa took it all by then
all those half breed lands
ribbon lots not "properly bought" were sold
and my ancestral uncle's home was pulled
up from under him like a rug

rolled up from the river's edge
all the way to the road
tucked under Canada's collective arm
and chucked on a eastbound train
with all the other rugs
all the other
rolled-up land
became tidy
cylindrical tokens
conquered
presents to be presented
to John A
nothing more than
rolled-up grass like pressed cigars
he lit up and smoked
'til they were spent
only white
ash brushed off
red coats
and made
nothing

2.

there is still a place called Vermette
just southeast of Winnipeg
still along the Seine
it has
a postal code
a store and a sign because
they let us use the names of our dead
as if that means
we're allowed to honour them

we do not forget our dead
we know where they are
and sometimes we pull
them out of the ground like relics
we brush them off
wonder at their possibility
like rotting bulbs of some
rare and fragile orchid
we tend to them
all winter
put them back
into the earth come spring
with nothing
more tangible than hope to
make them flower

our names are scattered
seeds all over this

mother land
fathers' names
sons' names

Ritchot
Beliveau
Beaupre

just words long lost of meaning

Dumont
Desjarlais
Debuc
Leduc

south side street signs
markers

Tourenne
Turenne
Traverse
Trembley

this city is a graveyard

Guimond
Guiboche
Guibault
Gautier

my "conquered" people
these children of bereft sons who
once thought themselves so grande
they had the nerve to create
a province

Carriere
Charriere
Chartrand
Côte

dead names breathing
thin dusty life

and Riel
Riel
everywhere Riel

we are intertwined within
this city
as if we belong
as if we are honoured

bury me at Batoche

bury me at Batoche
where their old shacks still stand
paint peels from weathered wood
but inside they smell like sweetgrass
sound like whispers

bury me behind them
in the graveyard where
stones hinge clouds
and the South Saskatchewan River
where wooden crosses
tilt to the sun
and wind answers
in a language I only know
in my bones but
every name is family
I can still hear them
they crowd around the fiddle
they dance gentle in the grass

bury me there
past the gift shop
and walkway where
quotations decorate
pixelated photos of dead men
and the story is shown at the top of every hour
same film used for two languages
over dubbed both ways so

both look like they're not
coming out of those mouths right

bury me in the shadow of the church
with its round flower window
bury me there 'cause that's where Grandmère will be
she will light candles
for those who went before us
but I'll just stay out here
and wait

where I can still see them
down in the coulees
their gun barrels pointed East
rough men in dirty shirts
whose sleeves billow like worn flags
rifle iron scrapes
and red coats shout
on the horizon
bury me here
where everyone lost
and everything changed
behind the new cast iron fence that shines
welcome to the graveyard along the river
a marble pillar notes a history in
Cree first
before French
before English

put me in the back
where most headstones are hand carved
fallen over but propped back up
where water rumbles like hunger
and birch leaves still dance
in the sun

long winter poem

1.

if I ever get to see you I will
open my hands to yours I will
close my dry
chapped fingers around
your thumbs I will
trace your long
telling fate line
with my bitten down
fingertips

if I get to see you I will
open my door
lead you in I will unzip
your winter coat and close
my strong tired arms around
you I will
hold you so tight you might think
I won't ever let go

2.

I miss you
these nights have fallen
first a sprinkle then
a shower now
a constant
downpour

in my dreams I have
told you all the things you have needed
to hear
when you get here
no words
will be important enough
to say

except I miss you
I miss you

you have the softest hands

I write you into every word every

I write you into every word every
noun and every verb
every syntactical choice
has something of you
lodged within it

I write you into every word every
time a metaphor leaps
or a simile jumps
like a frog
off a lily pad leaving
only a brief quiver
in the water
you are
that quiver

I write you into every word every
letter every sign each
line
break that hinges
in the middle of a thought
or a hesitation — a dash
that shoots off
the end —
an immediacy that runs
— both ways

I write you into every word I write
you into every

thing so
do not fear if I never
wrote your name
framed a character
in your shadow
or penned a sonnet
about your imperfect brown eyes the ones
I plunged into
and never
came out

flip over any sentence unearth
the simplest phrase
and you will find
pieces of you in it
bite-sized morsels
all the more
delicious because
they are broken

an other story

this country has an other story
one that is not mine
or yours
but ours

it is sung
from the mountains
danced in the sky
every star
a story
that teaches
hold your head up
wisdom
descends

this country has another story
not just for you
or me
but us

it is a prayer
I say to you
every word
burns hope
every silence
only peace

hold me tight
close the distance

between us
keep me
warm

acknowledgements

"black river" was written while visiting Little Black River First Nation, where my partner was teaching and is also a band member. I want to thank the community for welcoming me as a visitor so many times. I also want to thank Patricia Ningewance, beloved and prolific language teacher and writer of the book *Talking Gookom's Language*, which is referenced in these poems. Zaagi'idiwin.

"red river" was written while contemplating and then shooting the short film *this river* (NFB 2016). There are so many people to thank for this project, but especially Kyle, Alicia, erika, Iris, Anita, Calvin, Bernadette, and Ko'ona. That film and this section are dedicated to those who have been lost, and their loved ones who never stop searching for them — with the biggest love and absolute, eternal hope.

"an other country" comes from many places: Ottawa, Northwestern Ontario, Batoche, Winnipeg, Edinburgh, and more. Big thanks to the Outriders Project and the incomparable Harry Giles.

Several of these poems have been previously published in *Red Rising, Kimiwan, CV2, Prairie Fire, Rhubarb, Ricepaper, Cordite, Arc,* and *Taddle Creek*. "pieces" was a part of the Downtown Winnipeg BIZ–sponsored art project *Love* (2015) and is still on display on Portage Avenue; a section of "this river" was a part of the Wall-to-Wall mural festival (2017) and is up at the Tallest Poppy restaurant on Sherbrook Street (also in Winnipeg); and "When Louis Riel Went Crazy" was selected for *The Best Canadian Poetry in English 2018* (Tightrope Books).

Thank you to all who have read and helped with these poems — especially, but not limited to, Joanne, Gwen, and

Clarise. Big love to my editor, Damian, manager, Marilyn, and everyone at Anansi.

Thank you to the Manitoba Arts Council, the Carol Shields Writer-in-Residence program (U of W), and the Arnold and Nancy Cliff Writers-in-Residence program (UBC).

These poems have evolved over several years, so I am sure I forgot something or someone. If I did, I am so sorry. Thank you to everyone who has believed in me and my work. Writing is such a lonely job, but in it, I have found a community that makes it all worthwhile.

Maarsii to this land that holds us, to the waters that keep us, and to all who have come before and made the path I walk upon.

Finally, to my family — chi miigwetch. Giizhaweniiwin. Always. Forever.

katherena vermette is a Métis writer from Treaty One territory, the heart of the Métis nation, Winnipeg, Manitoba, Canada. Her first book, *North End Love Songs* (The Muses Company), won the Governor General's Literary Award for Poetry. Her NFB short documentary, *this river*, won the Coup de Coeur at the Montreal First Peoples Festival and a Canadian Screen Award. Her first novel, *The Break*, is the winner of three Manitoba Book Awards, the Burt Award for First Nations, Inuit, and Métis Young Adult Literature, and the Amazon.ca First Novel Award. It was also a finalist for the Governor General's Literary Award for Fiction, the Rogers Writers' Trust Fiction Prize, and CBC's Canada Reads.